Texting

Keep Your Relationship Exciting By Grabbing His Attention With Dirty Talk

(Sexting Strategies For Love Romance And Relationships)

Kristen Leblanc

Published By **Andrew Zen**

Kristen Leblanc

Texting: Keep Your Relationship Exciting By Grabbing His Attention With Dirty Talk (Sexting Strategies For Love Romance And Relationships)

ISBN   978-1-998769-28-5

No part of this guidebook shall be reproduced in any form without permission in writing from the publisher except in the case of brief quotations embodied in critical articles or reviews.

Legal & Disclaimer

The information contained in this ebook is not designed to replace or take the place of any form of medicine or professional medical advice. The information in this ebook has been provided for educational & entertainment purposes only.

The information contained in this book has been compiled from sources deemed reliable, and it is accurate to the best of the Author's knowledge; however, the Author cannot guarantee its accuracy and validity and cannot be held liable for any errors or omissions. Changes are periodically made to this book. You must consult your doctor or get professional medical advice before using any of the suggested remedies, techniques, or information in this book.

Upon using the information contained in this book, you agree to hold harmless the Author from and against any damages, costs, and expenses, including any legal fees potentially resulting from the application of any of the information provided by this guide. This disclaimer applies to any damages or injury caused by the use and application, whether directly or indirectly, of any advice or information presented, whether for breach of contract, tort, negligence, personal injury, criminal intent, or under any other cause of action.

You agree to accept all risks of using the information presented inside this book. You need to consult a professional medical practitioner in order to ensure you are both able and healthy enough to participate in this program.

Table Of Contents

Chapter 1: Texting Secrets Revealed

I will share a few secrets about dating that have been proven to work with all types. These secrets have helped hundreds upon scores of women to find their Mr. Perfect, which also allows the men to woo these women.

Let's begin to look at these secrets one after another.

Make the first move

Always be the first to move. It is important for women to realize that the majority of men take control. He will be just like you in your nervousness and most men don't want to take that step if it doesn't make sense. You don't have to wait for him, so start the conversation yourself. Be casual and friendly, such as "hi" or "how are you?" He might not respond right away if you say something casual and flirty like "hi, how are you?" If you send a simple "Hey!" message, chances are that he won't remember about it.

Make a Statement

This does not mean that statements are impossible to make. When you think something is true, say it. Don't even ask a question. Instead of asking the question "How was your morning?" tell him that "Hey, I'm sure it was a great one". If you feel confident enough, reply to him in advance: "I'm also having a great day." Try to keep your language light and flirty, but add some cute words like "Hey cutie, I'm having a great day!"

Cheese-with Limits

The common belief that all men are "nononsense" is widespread. They don't want to be treated like a baby. While most men enjoy hearing cheesy stuff, they need to know their limits. If you do decide to use some cheesy phrases, be sure that you only use them when it is appropriate. For example, you might not say "I have been thinking about" but instead you could say, "You've run around in my mind all day, those legs hurtin' yet?" You can also use these cliches by adding a twist.

Be responsible

Don't forget that most men enjoy being treated with affection. Men love it when you compliment them and talk to 'em. They love it when you reply to every question they ask and are honest with them. You can answer his question "Were there thoughts of me today?" by replying immediately "Yes!" You were there all day!" If you were busy, reply "Yes!" Although I was very busy, you remained in my mind for a long period of time." If you're looking to hook up with a guy that is really your type then you should reply to his messages as quickly as possible.

Show Care

Men love to be cared for. Even if he is someone you just met, and you want to spend time with him again, it is important that he sees that you care about him. Ask him questions such as "Hey, how are your teeth feeling?" or "Hey! How did you deal? with that mean boss of mine?". This will make it appear that you truly care about what's going on in his world.

Be a Thinker Before Him

Men tend to love and relate more to women who think ahead. To score a man you have to think ahead. If you are going to start a conversation, be sure you understand what is coming your way and you're ready to quickly give the answers. He will be taken by surprise, and will feel a greater respect for you. You can also ask him questions that are obvious to you and have an auto reply ready. You can also assess where he is at the moment with his questions, and then come up with new strategies.

Emoticons and Smileys

Smileys are charming and fun, and men love them. Just send a smiley when you're unsure. You can not only send a smiley to your friend, but it will also help increase his curiosity. You can send a smiley to him when you are unable to answer his question. Send him a string or smileys if you are insistent that he knows. You should not send two meaningless smileys. The smileys with the most impact are the simple smile --J, the smile --:* and blush smileys.

Humor and humor

Witty women are loved by men. If you start to realize that they are bimbos, they will stop messaging. Bimbos can be beautiful, but men will never want to get in bed or flirt with one of these women. Your ability to communicate clearly and intelligently is essential. It should include all the right words, and make sense. Use humor sparsely. If you're feeling silly, you can say funny and cute things while still being sane.

Chapter 2: Learn How To Make Your Girl Love You By Text.

You've done great so far. You have messaged the girl you love to say hi and that it was nice to chat. She has responded! You find yourself in panic and unsure of what to do next. It is important to be realistic. I will give you a few examples.

"I'm so glad that you replied. Since the time we met, I've thought a lot abou you. It was a good party.

Or, you can try this.

"Thanks so much for your reply. Your friends have told me nothing but good things about your company. Haha, I'm sure you've heard some good things about my personality.

Or...

"Yay. I've been waiting to hear back from you. I will be attending the football match tomorrow. Maybe we can catch up or chat a bit here.

You'll notice that these sentences are all very short and not too lengthy, are flirtatious yet not overtly flirtatious, have a fun ending and each one ends with a question. It is easy to ask a girl questions. Your questions need not be too personal or intrusive.

Be aware that she may feel anxious about your text conversation. Being yourself, friendly, humorous, kind, and respectful will allow her to do the same. It is important that you understand that her concerns about texting are likely the same as yours.

Let's bring up these concerns and discuss ways to address them.

* I am going on to be a bore.

* How can she keep my attention?

* What if you don't have something to say?

* My spelling and grammar are awful!

* I'm not funny or good-looking enough for her.

Let's not forget about boredom. But you don't have to be boring. You are unique because you have something that makes each person different. Don't let her know your insecurities when you talk to her. You shouldn't say things like "Oh, gosh, it's boring me," or "Oh, God, I hope it's not boring you!" Don't do that! Think confidently.

If you love each other, it is easy to keep your attention. Talk to her about your favorite things, and ask her about the ones she enjoys. Either you and she will discover you have lots of things in common that makes conversation easy or you are not right for each others.

Feel like you don't have something to say. You can be an amazing listener on text. Talk to her about yourself and show interest in the things she's saying. Listening to girls is a great way to show your interest. But you should be kind and respectful.

What if you're a bad speller. You have spellcheck! Your phone and laptop can be set up to do automatic spellchecks.

It's fine to make some spelling errors, though. However, if she does make spelling mistakes, don't laugh at her.

You know that feeling of not being good enough? It has nothing to do with the girl but everything to do about your own self-worth. Find happiness with who you really are and be proud of the things that make you unique. She will also notice these positive traits. Avoid focusing on the negative.

Avoid being annoying with text.

You are now feeling great after you have completed the first couple texts. Now you need to go beyond just the hello and the glad she replied bits. You also want to be flirtatious. You will need to pay attention to how she responds to you.

Avoid moving too quickly, as this could cause her to put you off. You should be playful, not flirtatious.

So, how do you have fun? Let's assume you have to work and are unable to text during your work day. At lunchtime, you could exchange a quick, playful and flirty message.

"Hey! I don't know if you need to respond because I know you are working but - it is hot, the day almost over and I wanted you to know that I am thinking of you!"

She will either respond telling you that she cares about you, or with an emoji. Do not try to get her to respond if she doesn't.

Maybe you could try this:

* "Hi there. I have the most delicious stake for lunch. Hopefully next week, or soon, you will be able join me.

If she is vegetarian, it's possible to serve the dish with a salad.

If you don't feel like you have to rush and are able send lengthy texts back, then you can think of other things you enjoy such as watching movies. You can ask her any questions you want, but she will not be interested in your private conversations. You might have finished watching Succession, and though you like it, the Sopranos is your favorite television show. Ask her what TV programs she likes or what movies she loves, and then tell her what your favorite movies are. These are easy conversations to have.

If you are looking to be flirtatious, you might suggest that you sit down together on the couch and watch a series. This could be a great way to make her feel edgy, playful and appealing. If you're not feeling a flirtatious vibe, it is important to

pay attention and be observant.

You can also send your girlfriend short, sharp text messages throughout the day. This will help you make her feel good, give her something positive to think about, give yourself a purpose in sending texts, and eventually, maybe get you to ask for a date.

Some examples of short, sharp texts include:

* "Oh my gods, you won't believe whom I bumped into!" Woody Allen!"

* "I thought about you all day. I hope your exam went well."

* "I am taking a 15 minute break, and thinking of you. Here is a cute dog clip."

* "Okay. This must be the cutest kitten meme I've ever seen!"

* "Superman just appeared in my hood. I want to see it. Date night

You should also make sure the messages you send her have a purpose. It's not enough just to say hello, or talk about weather. Your texts can cause annoyance to girls. Sending random texts is not the best way to communicate with a girl. You want to send a text which will lead you to a date. This is what you really want with her. It is important to be purposeful in your text messages. You want her expressing your admiration for her. This will allow you to tell her:

* "I cannot resist it, but you are beautiful!"

* "I'm so blessed that I've met the prettiest and most intelligent girl in the neighbourhood!"

* "Will this help if i tell you that i am really crushing right now? ?"

These are quite honest texts. But that is something else I want to discuss. Sexting should be avoided. You should not do this with someone you are really in love.

It will go stale faster than you can imagine, and you'll ruin something that could have been great. Sexting is passé. To be fair, it bores most girls. You should not be in a relationship if sexting is part your relationship.

Communicate with purpose. It doesn't necessarily mean you should ask the girl out on every text. You're building up to this, so ensure that she knows you are keen. Or else you might be friend zoned. You don't want to be friend zoned from a girl you love.

Avoid being friend zoned. You need to clarify some things at the beginning without getting pushy. Try:-

* Naomi, I am texting you because i like you a lot. Hope to have you as a friend.

* "Dominique. Even though I had only met you for a couple of minutes, I am

still thinking about you. Although it sounds absurd, let us chat!

* "I believe that we share a lot and I want you to know that, I like your. That shouldn't be a problem.

Chapter 3: General Tips

It is very easy to make a girl fall in love with you if that's what she wants. But, if not, it's important to find effective ways for her to learn about you and to eventually be with you. It is important to be resourceful. Researching her is essential. Also, you should seek out advice from your friends. These people will be able to help you understand her personality, as well as her likes. So that you don't give the impression of being a stalker, it is not necessary to be explicit when gathering this information.

Sending her text messages about her hobbies and favorites is another way to get interest. For example, let's say she likes Italian cuisine. Text "Hey, i know a nice Italian eatery near your home." Would you like to go with me to try their futtanesca This isn't an opening statement, but it does show how to be direct.

You could say that she's a very sporty girl. You could text her about your favorite sport or about her workout routine. Or compliment her on how toned her body. You don't have to be too specific or creepy.

A funny text message or joke can be another option. It is well-known that nearly all girls enjoy jokes. Girls are more likely to like guys who make their day brighter and make them laugh. A guy who is funny and witty is the best. A guy with a good sense of humor can make girls feel happy.

It can be a good idea to keep a positive attitude. This will make girls interested. Talk about a wonderful deed, or how beautiful the day was. Happiness is something girls always want.

Sending her funny pick-up lines can help you get her attention. It makes a girl laugh and smile, regardless of its absurdity. It also shows girls how clever you are by creating original pickup line designs.

Talk about family, but do not go overboard. Talk about family and share some of the traditions and happy memories you have with your family. Tell her how much you value your mom and how your dad inspires you. It could help you show your mom that you are also planning to start your own family. Women enjoy touchy-feely ideas. But don't overthink it.

Sending her a few text messages at a stretch and then ending the conversation can suffice to spark curiosity. It's possible to say you have something you want to do and that you'll text her later. She may be curious if you don't tell her what it is that you're going to do.

Chapter 4: How Technology Has Not Changed Dancing

Even though there have been many changes over the years in relationships and dating, there are still some fundamentals. Before we go on to discuss the things that haven't changed, let us talk about some texting tips. These rules are important for all types of relationships.

Girls and guys think differently. I know you are thinking "Duh!" Sometimes, girls forget this while texting guys. He doesn't care about the details of your shopping spree or the color you purchased. Most guys don't want endless chit chatting.

One thing hasn't changed: You should still allow the guy to ask you out. You may have heard that it is now acceptable to ask your man out. According to social standards, this is likely true. Mike (and nearly all guys) are honest. He wants to be the follower, no matter how old-fashioned it might sound. By appearing too eager, you risk compromising his natural desire and making it harder for him to pursue. You want him putting in effort to pursue you!

We will be talking more about building attraction later in this guide.

Does it sound like I'm suggesting you play a game with all this? You are actually playing a game. You're not married or even dating this guy. You're only trying to create tension and desire that leads you to him. That's not what you do by sending him a text shortly after meeting him. He doesn't have time to think about you, or what you thought about him. He doesn't have to impress you with his cleverness. What's your challenge? It's gone! You are the one who made them go away!

Smarten him up and let him know that you're willing to pay attention. A little patience and good timing will help you "get in" a guy's mind when it comes to texting - but only in a positive way!

Chapter 5: How Venus And Mars Communicate

It would be no surprise to discover that communication between men and females was not the same back then, if one could access a time machine. Even though our society has over 6000 languages, communication between the genders remains a challenge. Communication is seen by men and women differently.

Men communicate to pass on information. They are able to exchange information and do not feel the need to repeat themselves after it has occurred. Ronald D. Smith, communications professor, states that women communicate to create intimacy. The possibilities of conversation for them are limitless because they use communication to communicate, connect, and share.

While women use texting to make friends, men use it for more social activities like playing with their friends or going out with them. For men, texting is not the preferred method for communication when it comes intimacy. A woman may interpret a lack of texting by a man as a sign that the man does not want to be intimate with her.

The game is changing when it involves seduction by texting. A part of this includes the way in which men may alter their way of using text as a means of communication and use it for intimacy, rather than the traditional exchange-of-information way.

How to Text Women To Get Attracted

If you skip the first few chapters, and jump straight to this section, it is likely that you failed at seducing a woman via text. Don't worry! It happens to the best of us all.

You may have sent her an email but not received a reply. Or maybe you just felt like the conversation was getting stale. This illustrates how powerful texting can make a difference. One single text message can be all it takes to make her want to meet you again or to even get to know your family better. While texting can be easier than sexing with women, there are still some things that you must remember if your goal is to get any success.

Let's discuss the mistakes you may have made before we start to look at the right things.

You didn't complete your homework

Many men make the error of asking women for their numbers with too much confidence and overcompensating. They don't realize that they might be making a woman feel pressured into giving their number. Then they get surprised when they don't receive a response. You need to let her know that you'd like to see her again. But if she is not interested, you can tell that she isn't serious. It is important to express your intentions clearly. This is an example of how to do it:

"Claire. It was so nice to meet you. I have to leave right now. However, I will text you this weekend to let you know that we can either catch a film or eat at this Mexican restaurant. What do your thoughts? By doing this, you don't pressure her. You have let her make a choice and allowed her to choose.

You Thought Inside The Box, Not Outside

Many people don't have the ability to think clearly. How many times has that text message been sent to a woman? Your approach should be different and unique. Your approach should be based on the conversation you had with her just before you were offered her number. Remember that conversation in your first text.

You were your own worst enemy

Even though it sounds crazy, it is possible to be positive and confident while you write your first text message. When you think confidently, it is easier to write confidently. We are often afraid to doubt ourselves. Do not allow doubt to creep into your mind while you write the text.

You Said To Much

Text messages should not be longer than one sentence. You should not use text messages for conversation if your intention is to use them as a method of seduction. When you attempt to seduce a woman with positive personality traits and talking about them, there won't be much to talk about. Do not try to speak with her via text messages. This will demonstrate to her that you have more to do than text messages and keep her curious to hear more about you in a conversation.

You Thought You Were Romeo

Do not send text messages with too much romance too soon, regardless of what you may think. You might have thought that she would see you as sweet and caring and that it would make her feel more loved than a box Nevada dessert chocolates. Wrong! She will not be seduced by you. Instead, she will make fun of you and her friends as she shares romantic messages and poems with her. Keep the cheesiness to yourself.

What you should do

It should be fun to text a woman that interests you. It should not be about trying to get her into bed or manipulating her. Women will be attracted to men who are happy-go-lucky or have fun around them. Even if you're naturally shy, this can give a boost.

In a sense, the first text reads more like an ad. Your time and space are limited to make a lasting impression. You can think back to some of the greatest commercials you've ever seen. They were the same as every other commercial. No! They offered something new and different. It was because they listened carefully to their audience, and created something that would grab their attention. You should follow this approach and not get too focused on it. What are some ways to do this?

Use the information you have on the person

One of the most common complaints women have about men, is their inability to listen. If you want to stand out from other guys, it's worth asking her about something that she mentioned. Maybe she mentioned that her desire to see a specific play or that she needed a new dress. It might be worth contacting her first to discuss it.

"Hi Mandy. How was your dress-hunting experience?" What was your experience with finding something special?

After she responds, you could add: "That seems very pretty. Aren't you planning on wearing it when you go see (insert the name of the play)"?.).

This is a great way to open the door to potential dates.

Keep your eyes focused on the prize

Because women enjoy chatting more than men, it's very common to find women who text only for the pleasure of it. This is fine if the goal of your friendship zone is to keep in touch with them, but if this is your main objective, it's best to meet up immediately to discuss your goals and determine if it is worth continuing your pursuit.

Avoid using text to set the first date

You can set up a date with your best friend by sending a text message if you want to meet someone close to you. If you want to set the date for the woman who you have been trying unsuccessfully to seduce, a simple phone call will suffice. It will make her feel like you are a man and show her you have the confidence to do it over the phone. You must think confidently, get to the point quickly and remain calm. Remember, you have other tasks to complete.

Laugh and the entire world will be laughing with you

A man who has a sense of humor is irresistible is what women love. A man who takes himself seriously but can make his woman happy is likely to be in love with her. Sarcasm should be avoided from the start. It is important to feel her senses of humor. It can be very helpful to include emoticons in your messages, especially since she is unable to see your cute smile.

Read a book instead of playing Xbox

Many women believe the brain is the most seductive part of a male. While you don't need to have an IQ over 150 to seduce a lady, it can help you keep up-to-date on current affairs. Or at least watch documentaries if your passion is reading. You should use what you have learned to text in a subtle way, but not give too much away. This is something that you can use to have a conversation with someone on a actual date.

How to seduce men using texting

You may have assumed that seducing man was easy. However, you would still enjoy the chapter. Contrary to what you were taught by your mother, it's not always as simple as "the only way to a woman's heart is through their stomach". You know that the seduction game has changed. This is especially true in women. Why?

* If you send a message to a friend, you can be sure he has seen it.

* You don't have to dress up in order to text your boyfriend. You can sit in your pajamas, with morning breath, and still have the ability to blow his socks!

* You can start to build chemistry by texting before you actually meet him in person. In the past this was impossible.

But now, you have the chance to create a potential relationship on their terms.

* Men respond to what you paint with their words. Texting gives you the opportunity to think ahead and craft a highly seductive message.

Remember to always have an end in mind when messaging men. Many women make the omission of being fully transparent about their desires. Be clear and specific about what you want. There are other guidelines that will assist you in your seduction strategies.

Play hard ball

It may sound obvious to say that playing hard-to obtain might seem like a wise thing to do, but many forget that texting is just as important as real life interaction. It is important to always be one step ahead and convince him that he is actually seducing you.

The best reply is to not reply at all

The best strategy to add to your arsenal of texting techniques is to make him wait until you reply. If you send him a message that you expect a specific response to, even the most confident of men will make all sorts of assumptions. Be sincere when you reply. Don't make excuses like "Oh sorry I didn't get your message." You want to create tension that will lead to attraction.

You are not his mother

Any man does not want to hear: "Where have your been?" or "Haven't you been getting my messages?". This is the best way to drive a man away. You will remind him of his mother's old treatment of him as a baby. It could make him feel desperate or needy.

Give him the paintbrush and let him draw.

To get a man attracted to yours, you can create a blank canvas in your mind and let him draw the picture. Nonchalantly answer his questions by telling him what you've been doing. Be flirty and sexy. Not slutty. Try saying something like, "I was just in a shower and I thought about you." He will have to ask you why you thought about him.

Keep it short and make it enjoyable

However sincere you may be, asking a guy his day will make him feel like it's a burden to answer this question. Keep it simple. Men use communication to send messages, as I mentioned in this book. One example is "Hey, I was thinking of you." Would you like to try a new Italian restaurant in the next week? If you're going on a date, the questions you have for him are more broad. You also managed to build anticipation with this date by using "later this weeks" without revealing a specific date or time.

Chapter 6: Texting Strategies To Keep Him Interest In You

Apart from using the strategies described in the previous section of this guide, once you have his attention and he is starting to feel a connection for you, it is important to put yourself into his mind and heart. You can also use these strategies to keep him interested.

7 Texting strategies that will keep him interested

Here are some texting tips to keep your interest and keep him reading:

#11 - The 80/20 Rule of Texting

Now that you have his interest in your company piqued, he is eager to increase things, you need to remember the golden rules of attraction and getting a woman to fall in lust and love you: the power to chase. If he doesn't feel as though he is chasing and winning you over, it will be a sign that he is not interested in you.

You can prevent this from happening by using the 80/20 rule for texting. The 80/20 Rule of Texting simply refers to finding a healthy equilibrium between the moment a message hits your inbox, and the moment that you reply.

The rule says that for 80% of your messages, you should wait --two times as long as you would normally expect to wait--before you start texting him. For 20%, you should immediately text him back or as soon as you can.

This strategy is simple, but it works. It forces you to be unpredictable. That makes him more competitive.

#12 - Text blackouts will keep him connected

Intelligent text blackouts are a way to keep your client interested in your message communications and hooked. It allows you to text him for short periods, but not text, so that he is always interested.

Allow him to text you for a short time, or marginally longer, but do not respond.

Because you will be more appealing and valuable if you are genuine with your responsibilities, the general working day is a great period of blackout. You can also use text blackouts for Friday evening or most of the weekends.

Text blackouts increase his curiosity, interest, and because he will still wonder about you during these periods, he is likely to remain interested enough in you to want to escalate the correspondence into a date.

#13 - Clever emoji to add flavor

Emojis aren't for men. It doesn't mean they shouldn't be used or that they don't appreciate clever use of emojis.

Use emojis whenever you feel it is appropriate, but not when they are necessary to emphasize the meaning and intent of your text. Avoid becoming emoji-crazed by sending only emoji reply messages. If he feels snubbed, it will greatly reduce his interest.

It is a good rule of thumb to match his demeanour with emojis. If he doesn't use emojis in text messages, then emojis in your texts will look sophomoric. This will reduce his interest and decrease his desire to communicate with you. It is a good rule to limit their use to text that adds an intentional layer. Here is a playful example of flirtatious emoji: "I don't want to miss you."

#14: Stringed messages will get your nowhere

Common texting mistakes made by women who truly love a guy include sending him stringed texts messages. These are text messages that are sent in a sequence and not returned by the man. This type of texting error is not recommended.

No matter how much you want to text him, he will not respond to your texts. This will make you appear desperate for him.

If you want to text him, wait for him to respond before you start texting again. This will make it impossible to text him again. Also, you should not send him too many text messages when he hasn't responded. This will defeat the purpose of steps 11-12. He might be attending a meeting, or just busy with his own life.

#15 - Ace the timing

This step is identical to the previous.

We assume that the man who is interested and attracted to you is a driven, high quality man. Text correspondence is not easy. He too is busy working, just as you are.

It is important to learn his schedule so that you are able to text him when he's not busy. Texting him at 10AM will help you get his attention.

If you're texting him during work, it is a good idea to keep him informed by text messages.

#16 - Grumbling texts can get you ignored

Women also make the common mistake of sending complain text messages. For example, if your workday isn't going as planned, you may succumb to the temptation to send him a series of complaining texts.

This type of sharing is perfectly acceptable. It is best to only share your feelings when you feel that the relationship has gone beyond just attraction.

This stage of attraction is too early to send him messages complaining about his boss, your bosses, your sassy girlfriends or the rotten sandwich he bought.

Sending him such texts shows that you don't really have anything to share with him. It also diminishes your worth and increases the chance of him being ghosted. It is important to remember that good banter is the best way for you to get anywhere.

#17: The teasingly suggestive text will make his blood boil

To keep him on his toes all day (and at night), send him teasing text messages that are filled with curious questions and statements. These messages will leave him hungry for more.

Keep in mind that although men are drawn to the 'chase', you need to offer him something to chase. The best way to do that is to send him text messages. You can also use suggestive statements and questions to get him in a frenzy and make it seem like he's ready to go on a date.

Be gentle and flirtatious. He will be more likely to reciprocate. For example, you could send a text message saying, "Want a glimpse of how flexible I am?" This message will cause his mind to spin as if in a hamster wheels and result in you likely receiving an equally suggestive reply.

You must keep your messages sexy, flirty and sexy for him to remember what you said. This will be covered in more detail in the next section.

Chapter 7: Sexting In Relationships

You may not have known that sexting can make or break a relationship. It is possible to spark a carnal desire for someone by sending a few messages that are short and simple. You can read this chapter to learn more about how sexting helps build intimacy between a couple.

Numerous experts suggest that sexting builds intimacy. Research shows that text messages that contain explicit or flirtatious language are most often sent by people adding images. Sexting can be a great way to build intimacy and strengthen a couple's bond. It gives you the opportunity to express yourself to your partner, in a way you might not otherwise, and thus builds trust and bonds that are not there. You can use the sentiment for people who are either single or in a committed relationship.

Some parents may feel nervous about the process, as they could be sitting alongside their child while they receive a sexual orientation. This could raise ethical questions. The answer to your question, "Is it okay to send an e-sext while you go out to lunch with your child?" is yes. Yes. It isn't like your child is reading explicit texts or looking through your phone. If your older children look at your phone, this book can provide you with some helpful warnings.

Sexting can be used as a form foreplay for couples who feel bored in the bedroom. These couples can "get going" together by sexting during the day and then going to bed for a late-night session in the bedroom.

Gender Divide

There are differences in the way that technology and intimacy affect genders. Men are usually less verbal than females. A woman may wish her man would pick-up a phone but texting will make him feel more in control. If you think it sounds like psychology, it's probably true. It is common knowledge that men think

differently about relationships.

A University of Nebraska at Kearney sociology professor conducted a survey and found that both dating sites and social networking are built around matching men with women. The study found that two thirds (33%) of women on dating sites engaged in sexting. It also showed that the majority of sex sessions were initiated by men. This is similar to the texting of men. Also, this is true if you are female. Men are more interested in texting on a regular basis. You will therefore most likely start something that will be interesting to him.

Chapter 8: Don't Be A Terrorist Texter

This is another error most women make. Women hate that men don't reply immediately so they send more texts, which can lead to irritation.

Look at the below sample text messages to find out what is going wrong.

Hello, how are your?

What are you doing today?

Jennifer had a party on the weekend. You should be there.

What are you going to do next weekend?

You have not responded to my texts. Are you busy or not? Is there something that has happened to you, or someone we know?

What's happening?

What the heck is going on?

Why aren't your replies?

You need to have some balls! You don't really care about it, do you?

You see, this woman was so focused on getting a reply from her ex, she didn't realize she was being too pushy.

Yes, it is frustrating to be on both ends of a cold message or not getting a response. It is also important to remember that being a "text terrorist" won't help you in any way, as it will only make the other person more annoyed.

Remember that even if someone is awaiting your text, they wouldn't be waiting hand-in-hand. Everyone has a job. They have work, and they have things that must be done. Instead of waiting for someone texting them, they have something to do. Although it might be hard to resist sending too many messages, if it is your goal to get your ex back it's worth keeping the following in mind.

1. Consider your ex-partner's position. Do you really want to receive multiple texts from your ex every day? What makes you feel good? It gives the victim the impression that their ex is being obsessive. You also need to make sure he doesn't view you this way. If he does not respond right away, ask him again. Consider that he may simply be busy. Instead of acting as if you are his owner, remember that you don't.

2. It's not his duty to reply. He might feel like he's running away from your partner if you push him to answer. You can be casual about it. What would it mean to try and get him back if you did it within three days of the breakup? This would suggest that you're too excited about this. As I mentioned in the first chapter it doesn't have to be. Give him the chance of missing you. Give him the chance of wanting to receive a message from you. If you do this, you can be sure that he'll answer.

3. He may also be trying make up his mind. You can't force him to make a decision for you. He will have to reply if you ask him.

4. It doesn't mean you have to know everything. Okay, he doesn't respond. It doesn't give him the right not to answer.

You don't have to ask your boyfriend where he's at the moment, what he's doing, or why it isn't responding. Be a good girlfriend and not a clingy one. He won't want to be together again. Is this what you want? You are wrong!

5. Do not call the company to follow-up. Here you are not hiring employees. This is your ex. You're trying to reunite with him. You don't want him to change the number you have been calling him and sending texts. Obsessive behavior is not something you want to encourage.

These facts are now in order. Now it's time to learn which strategies you can use to text an ex.

Chapter 9: Watch Your Spelling

Many men are better at spelling than their female counterparts and place less importance on it. Misspelled texts can be very dangerous and you should ensure that everything is correct before you send it.

This is because spelling correctly is an indicator of your status. While you may think that it doesn't matter what your education or future career prospects, others can make judgments. Even if she isn't consciously considering your future together on an unconscious level, she will still look for clues in order to evaluate who you really are.

By nature, humans feel the need for categorizing people. It is natural and something that many people do not enjoy, but it is hard to avoid. All she knows about you and the text messages that you have sent is what she remembers from the time you got her number. A simple correction of a sentence or two is possible so take the time.

Tell a story

However, when I say you should tell an interesting story, I don't mean that you have to tell a long story. Not every text that you send out must be a query. The most common mistake men make is to get into interview mode. The same approach is used when talking to a female face-to face. They also use it in their text chat. The interview mode is something like this.

"So which college did y'all go to?"

"Does this song appeal to you?"

"Does anyone know of any brothers or sister?"

"What kinds of movies do you enjoy watching?"

In an attempt to fill the empty space with some conversation, many men resort to interviewing their female counterparts. If you think back to the interview situations you have had, was it a pleasant and easy experience? This is how you would talk with your family or friends. Both are almost impossible to answer.

This is why she doesn't need you to ask her a question every single time you send a text. Instead, tell her about your day or what just happened. Tell her what you saw and how it made your day. These texts will be more intimate than those you would send to friends and can create more intimacy. Because you've given her something to talk over, you're more likely get a response. It shows that your are not stuck at work or at home.

Have fun!

Women and men are alike in the fact that the primary reason we interact with and form relationships with each other is our desire to have fun. You're probably familiar with the long-term marriages that have lost their spark. This may be a pattern you see in your own family or from someone you know. We can see why almost half of marriages end up in divorce.

Nobody wants to live a life like this. People want fun and romance. A woman's most favorite fantasy is the one of the mysterious strangers. This is a man that appears out of the blue and sweeps them off their feet. The stranger who appears out of nowhere is exotic and far more powerful than life. You can live up to your fantasy if you know what to do.

When men start texting women they have just met, it is a loss of their greatest advantage, which was this unknowable quality. They send dull and irrelevant texts. These texts inform her that this man doesn't have the same interest in her as other men. She is looking for something more in her life, and you don't provide it.

Instead, make texting fun and exciting. Through the clues you leave in your messages, make sure she knows that you have lots going on. A number of factors contribute to women being attracted to rock stars, including their status and the fact that they are always in the spotlight. They have so much going on in life. They want to be enthralled in the excitement.

A person who doesn't have a life isn't someone anyone wants to date. You don't want to reply too quickly. If you can reply so quickly, you should not have too many other things going on. You don't hear back from her until tomorrow morning if she sends you a text message in the afternoon. "Sorry I didn't get back, my friend's group was in town and gave me backstage passes. I must have left my smartphone at home." It is an indication that you have lots going on in life. Then, she will almost be forced to send an email saying "It's alright ..."

Look at how you have altered her power relations. You have made it seem that she is more dependent on you than you are. She tried to reach out, but you were too busy. Your value will rise if you don't make yourself unavailable.

But I Don't Want to Lose Him

This is a major obstacle to sexual attraction via texts. The scenario is as follows: You are on Saturday night, and you call this adorable little blonde. You found her interested and enjoyed the conversation. You are aware that other men might also desire to date someone as attractive. It occurs to you that if she is comfortable talking to other men, it is likely she will also talk to other guys.

In other words, you don't want to lose your girlfriend. Keep going and you drive her away. She read what you thought was genuine interest and sincerity, as desperation. There was no mystery. She knew she could have your back. You are likely to have witnessed men be arrogant and disrespectful towards the women they are speaking to. Why do these jerks seem so attractive to women? They are not dependent.

To get girls you don't necessarily have to be a jerk. However, you can be nice and helpful, but not too needy. Text messaging should be fun and you must be willing for her to leave.

You won't get her even if it sounds zen. I said that you shouldn't reply for more than an hour or the entire evening if your goal is to create a feeling of inadequacy. If you do this, she may fall for another guy or decide that you're a jerk. We are only talking about one evening so it is very unlikely. You will come off as desperate if these chances are not taken.

Stay in control of the conversation

When meeting women, a common mistake men make is to allow women too much control over their conversation. Women love to talk so it is important to allow them to fill in the gaps. You want to have control over the topic and the speed at which the conversation progresses.

If you do not text her or wait a few days before she responds, there is a possibility she might get mad at you. Women value communication more than men. If you spend enough time with women, you will see how many text. This is a good sign if she does not tell you off. It's a good sign that she noticed you didn't text her, and that they are interested.

Don't assume you must change your behavior right away. It is not about building friendship but attraction. Sometimes what she tells you she wants and what attracts her are not the same thing. This is called cat string theory. It basically states that if you place a piece or string in front of your cat, she will keep reaching for it. The cat would be unable to grasp the string if it was given to them.

This universal desire to desire what we can't has isn't limited to women. Women are experts at this art, and can keep men interested by using it. It's the hot/cold issue. At times, she may seem interested but at other times, she might not. It can frustrate men but it will keep them engaged.

If you're using the same tactics as the women you want to pursue, then you will be the only one. You are playing games and manipulating situations, but you must ask yourself if this is what you want. At the end, you're creating attraction.

How to know if she's interested

What are known as indicators or interest? When we text a girl, we look for these clues. These are indicators that indicate whether the girl is open to a date, or if there is more to be interested. There will be times when we miss the signs. However, these will help to avoid making mistakes like asking too soon for a date or not asking if she is showing that she loves you.

Before we start to look at these indicators, one thing I would like to say. I would advise that you ask your girl out if you're not sure if she's interested in meeting you within a certain time period.

It is very difficult to build sexual attraction with texting. It's a good idea to ask her out. Most likely, if you believe she is going to decline you, you are correct. Men don't usually understand the signals sent by women so if you get them bored, it is likely she isn't. But, you will only know what you do when you try.

Double text is the best indicator of interest. A double-text is not a good indicator of interest. Sometimes, she will text you again if you do not reply to one of her texts. Although tone is important, she may also text you again if you send her texts with the following message: "Just wondering about your life / if my text goes through."

You can use a pattern break to make her stop texting twice. This allows you to set a pattern for how fast you send back messages. She may text you 15 minutes after you have replied. She begins to expect that you will return her messages quickly, even though she sent them herself. It is possible to break the pattern by not replying much later. Double-check that she texts you to confirm that she received your message. This is a good sign of interest because she was expecting your reply.

When you leave a woman wanting to make contact again with you, you're creating value. If we do not care about someone, then it doesn't matter if they get in touch with you quickly. Even if she doesn't know yet if they like you, if she has a feeling of expectation for your message, it is likely that she has a subconscious desire to be with you.

It is also a sign that she is interested and flirtatious in you if you receive texts from her. Some women are naturally flirtatious so it is important to not read too much until you get to know the woman better. It's been my experience that women who are naturally feisty are great to have fun with.

Remember that I said it was a good idea if you used a nickname to text her? It's a great sign when she makes up a nickname for yourself. The same way we use nicknames for intimacy and connection to make us feel closer, she will create a nickname specifically for you.

Unless humor is something you dislike, it's a good idea for you to start making jokes. If she responds well to your jokes, this is another indicator that she is interested. Your approach seems to work and you should continue with it. Not every text has to be funny. Texts that are clear and concise will work.

It would be a good idea for you to encourage the girl you are texting to show interest and invite her on a date.

Chapter 10: First Message After Getting Her Number

How long do you need to wait before texting her?

You may wonder how long to wait before you send her a text message after you get her number.

It is a common mistake for guys to leave it too late to send the first message. They don't want people to think they are needy. Although this is true, you can make these two mistakes if your texting back takes too long.

Firstly, she will start to forget about your name and may begin to talk to another person. You won't get her attention unless you make a lasting impression from the first meeting. High-quality girls will not wait for their men, because they will be offered elsewhere.

Secondly she will see through the game you are playing and lose your trust. It is far more dangerous for her to text too late that it is early. If you send a text to your girlfriend too late (e.g., more than a week), it is almost impossible to explain why or what you were doing.

If it was a friendly exchange, a good rule is to send her a text within 24 hours of the conversation while you are still fresh in their minds.

If you leave it too long, she might forget all about you. You can leave a little mystery or anticipation because she will be uncertain after the initial encounter whether you like her. If you text her, she'll think "oh, maybe he likes us" which keeps you guessing.

How fast you can message a girl depends on how successful the first interaction was. It's important to evaluate the situation. There is no mathematical formula that can tell you exactly how many hours and how many minutes to wait.

You might be better off not texting her if she mentions that she is about to go out to dinner with some friends. There are no reasons to not continue hanging out with her or text her during dinner.

Another example is to have a fluid conversation on a dating application and get her phone number to transfer the conversation between app and text. Then you can immediately message her. Do not wait until 4 hours later, as that is the norm. She's likely expecting you to message her once you've had a flow of conversation.

What's the first text message you should send to a girl in a text message?

The quality of the interaction will influence the message you send. If you feel that the interaction went well, and you have decided to meet again, then you can quickly go through the steps of texting. Your first text serves to organize the logistics for the date.

Example:

"Hey. It was great meeting you last night. It would be great if we could get together.

While you are showing her interest and being direct, you don't push for meeting up at a particular time. It's still very casual and open.

If the interaction went poorly, you'll have to go through the steps again. Add value, create comfort. You can start your conversation by reminding her about the initial interaction.

The formula for this is:

[Name] +[Reminder/compliment of You] + [Recap Of The Night]

Example:

"Hey! It's Jack. You were greeted by a dark, tall, handsome man from Canada.

This message is very special because it contains your name and a humorous reminder of who we are.

It assumes that the woman will remember you for how you described your self. Be playful with it. It doesn't necessarily have to be tall and dark or handsome. However, you can describe yourself in a humorous and amusing way.

You can begin to build your text record by seeing how she responds to compliments.

Chapter 11: Texts Which Are Turn Offs

You don't have to be clever with flirts or chats. There are also text messages that could turn off men. Bad texts can not only turn off a guy, but could even lead him to stop reading your messages.

You might be able to decipher texts that you have to use a codebook. One clever person created all these abbreviations, such as gr8. Phones now have keyboards. It is not necessary to continue writing the code.

Use of "lol" and "lmao is acceptable. Anything that is now so common that even your grandma understands its meaning is fine. However, don't try to be clever using abbreviations. It's easy to misunderstand text messages. As much as possible, stick to the real words.

Here are some other types of text you should avoid.

Necessity - Constant texting shouts NEEDY and DESPERATE. There is no better way to stop a guy from paying attention than by being anxious. Texting constantly is a sure way to keep a guy's attention. Not only will he not respond, but he might also move you to his "not worthwhile it" list.

I get it, it's hard to resist the temptation of sending a text message over and over again when they don't reply. Accept that he might be busy or not interested and will reply when he has time. If it's either the former, it means he's going to reply immediately. If it happens to be the latter, it doesn't matter if you send him more texts. Non-stop texts are pointless. In the worst case scenario, it's better just to keep your face clean and reduce your losses.

Whining – This doesn't work in person and is even more annoying in text. Don't do it.

One word texts – Ha or LOL. What if someone was actually speaking to you? The other person responds with "Ha" and makes a funny comment. That's it. Just, "Ha". And then it sat there waiting to hear your response. The conversation was essentially thrown back at you. The conversation must be two-way. It's important to make intelligent or interesting comments. Sometimes a single word answer is enough. When you are getting to know someone, it can be helpful to add to the conversation. Lol and OMG have been overdone. They should be avoided whenever possible.

Don't Always Be the First to Make Contact. - Even if you've been messaging for a while, it's OK to send the second text occasionally. Don't be the first person to send a message. This makes you appear clingy, desperate. Let him send you a text, then see if you reply. Or when and what information you'll give back to him.

ALL CAPS or tons of exclamation point - Why do you even need to explain it?

Bitchiness-There's a fine distinction between being edgy, and being bitchy. You can sometimes show your tough side. The kind of bitchiness and meanness that you display is not likely to attract the man you want to be with. Talking negatively about your ex's is a red flag. This shows that you judge your boyfriends and are willing to share negative opinions with other people.

Therefore, if your boyfriend is with you and you have a bad relationship, you'll be talking trash about him.

Serious discussions are not for texting. Don't say things like "We need a talk" or, "Do you think this relationship will go anywhere?". If you're just meeting someone, these conversations shouldn't be happening yet. These types of conversations are best if you have been dating for some time. Use the phone instead if this is not possible. For serious, long-lasting conversations, avoid using text messages. There's just too much room to misunderstand. It's tacky, too.

Breakups – You don't need to send someone a text to end your relationship. Ever.

Chapter 12: A Great Text's Nit And Grit

If you're face-to-face with a guy, women can do many things: twirl, show off cleavage, or lay their hands on his forearm. Texting takes all of that out of the equation. As you stare at your phone, you try to figure out which emoji is the best for you flirting. You get confused; you may even get a bit nervous. You send random messages, and you end up losing your mind. This is frustrating and common. Over the years, women have perfected flirting. Face-to face flirting is easy. We are able to read their body language like a book. Unfortunately, this is where the magic happens. Great flirty texts are all about creating tension. To create tension, it is important to stay one step ahead. This is how you can build your attraction. It makes them want more. It allows you the ability to inspire them with ideas and help them to think about what they might achieve. Attraction can only be created by wanting something that you don't have. Whatever it may be, a beautiful car, a boat or the perfect guy, you can attract them. It is a great drive knowing that it is challenging and that we will be in a position to achieve this. You need to create a short, punchy, and flirtatious text that hooks and reels in your recipient. This will help you build a rapport and spark a conversation. This will allow you to get to the bottom of his questions, and help you build a stronger relationship.

Once you have the number, send him a playful message. It will really draw him in. It is a good idea to take the time to think about what to say next. Then, consider all possible responses.

It is vital to never ask a yes/no question. Once you ask a yes/no question, you end the conversation. Nobody wants to hear "OK, cool!" and there is no place to go. To allow the other person to respond, and make it more conversational, leave it open. These are often the hardest questions to answer and the most difficult. You will also strengthen your relationship by forcing him to share this information. Always think before you send him a message. Do you want him to feel embarrassed or like you are pushing the boundaries? Always be polite. It is important to recognize when he is speaking up. This can be difficult, so be gentle and patient.

While text messaging is not the best place to start long, drawn out conversations about parent divorce or ex-partner problems, you can still discover some fascinating facts about your partner. They will also be more open to sharing their feelings with you because they know that they cannot see how you would physically react. This is very important and something you should have in your back pocket. It is okay to flirt with him by asking, "What do ya really think about me?" Don't be afraid of being too direct. He has the option to respond as he pleases. If he is so taken with your sexy texts that he gives an honest, relationship friendly answer, then he will.

Sometimes we are a little too optimistic, sometimes we can go too far.

Chapter 13: Flirtexting Messages To Get Things Moving And Some That Slam On The Brakes

Are there messages that seem to open up the flood gates? One message that will get you talking for hours. These are the messages that should be your goal.

Here are some flirtexting messages examples that can get the ball rolling.

* Unformatted text Wait! Wait! The other person will be sure to ask you about what is happening. You can then play clever and say, "My phone must think that I am thinking only of you ...".

* A follow-up message regarding something you were discussing in person. "Oh, yes, I remember what was going to say

* A cute text: "I dreamed about you" Or "I was thinking ..."

*

It is okay to send messages that are lighthearted and a little bit naughty, but it is important not to go overboard.

Brake Slammers

* Yes or no questions.

* Things too bizarre or uncomfortable to mention.

* Saying too much, to soon

The Awkward Reality Of A Response That Doesn't Go in the Right Direction

Texting away with the most epic message, there you are. You wait for fifteen minutes, then you get the reply "K. Cya." Wait. What?

You send a beautiful almost poetic message to your friend that took two attempts to create and you get this back. What is the matter?

Do you need to text your friends and start asking them questions? Are you supposed to be angry? Should you be upset? Should you feel worried, angry, and hurt all at once?

It's no! After you have calmed down, you should text "are you still busy?" and if they reply "no", you should ask if there is a way to speak with them.

If you are able to wait and discover what is going on in real life, it's even better. You can observe their reactions and facial expressions, which can often give you a greater clue about what they are thinking and feeling.

Five Types You Will Love About Flirtexting

Flirting has two goals: to win someone's affection and to keep it. You want others to see you as positive. These are the types that will bring you the interest you seek:

The confident, strong woman

This woman flirts with you by sending flirty texts. It shows that she is genuine and wants to be your friend. Use something like "Thinking Of Me?" You are now

Text him with "you know which I like best" as a description of the best part of the conversation or the most memorable moment. It should be something that is real and meaningful so your crush will not forget it.

The Teasing Text

It is fine to flirt, but it is not appropriate to say anything.

The I want everything about you texts

These are the texts asking questions. They should be friendly and lighthearted. Asking for personal information is not a way to interrogate someone.

The anticipation builder text

Texts like "Ooh when I see your again builds anticipation, and are very hot.

The types that might prevent things from going further.

The you are mine pal texts

"Sup?" Yep. You will see them falling in love right there at your feet. These texts send all the wrong messages, so they're not worth it.

The life story/woe me texts

It was a flirtex that led to a relationship. Stop if you have too many messages or your message is broken down.

You have sent a photo of your naked self

You have sent a photo of yourself naked to someone with whom you had briefly sex, perhaps even once or twice. He might think it's all fine, but it could not be.

What if you had the courage to discuss such topics? How do you know if this is appropriate at this point in your relationships? Remaining calm will pay off in long term.

The too restrictive text

You're now freaking out because he hasn't returned your calls in ten minute. You've texted "is that it?" and" "don't you love me anymore?" to someone to whom you haven't yet committed. With these messages, it's unlikely that you will ever get there.

People don't like feeling under constant surveillance or that everything is in order. Be that person.

The threat messages

You are sure that you have crossed a line. You are sure you've made a big mistake. So what should you do? Please accept your apology and suggest you start again. No!

Instead, your rage is all out and you continue to get worse.

If you are seriously considering suicide, call a hotline. If you do not take your situation seriously, you will be a horrible, awful individual. Your crush should run fast.

Chapter 14: A Positive Attitude In Dealing With Demotivating Reactions

This guide will give you the information you need to text a woman to make her yours. It is very important to be careful when writing your texts as ladies are sensitive about what you share. If you don't explain what you said, they may misunderstand pieces of information and use them to attack you. A girl's reaction to a text message or comment can make it seem different. As if you want to let her know that you're available. She can then get ready for a texting session with you, or just ask how your day has been.

Alternative texting: Your text should read something like "Hey Nish. It was great to have you as a friend, and I enjoyed the chat more than the coffee we had."

Enjoy a great evening and we look forward meeting again soon. Joe

It should arrive within 24 hours. Send a follow-up message after a dinner date within an hour to ensure she does not forget the evening. It's amazing how much conversation you have with your date will continue throughout the night. You can also let her know what you like and how you would like to see the relationship continue.

Sometimes, it is easy to doubt the feelings and motives of the lady you just met. You can send a brief text to let her know that you are okay with the time she gave you. If you notice anything that you didn't like about the dinner experience, like an absentmindedness call or confusion in the call, highlight it. Make it funny so she doesn't take it too serious and thinks you are being rude.

It is vital to bring up every interaction between you. Sometimes, it is just a typo or a slip of tongue. However, if you remain silent and do not make your own decision, it may turn into a nasty situation. Ask it politely and you'll be surprised at how pleasant your interaction will become. If you think it was a mistake, explain it and tell her that she has the right to ask any questions. Openness with each other is key to healthy relationships.

Dealing with negative reactions

The lady you're starting a relationship with will most likely have the tendency to cancel your plans. You can expect her to cancel dates or give you reasons she is unable to attend. Your attitude towards cancelling will influence her judgement. You must be positive about the situation and not feel hurt.

One example is that she might tell you that she won't show up because she is helping her friend with chores. Given that you had planned for the entire week to go on the date, it is not surprising that you are disappointed. Your reaction should not reflect that you are excited to meet her and have a great evening. Instead, you should be positive and pretend that you did not have other plans.

To the contrary, tell the friend that you want her to have a great time and show concern by saying she should take care. Tell her, however, that you want to steal her the next Friday as she is missing you a lot.

Men who are too possessive with girls can be very irritating to them. Text-based communication means that you can find comforting words to use when she brings up something negative. It is important to show your concern for her decision and that you are happy for her. When she is finished with her activities, you can bring her back to your full attention.

However, if you really want her there at the prearranged time, do not ask it in such a way as to suggest that you are merely waiting for her enjoyment. You will not get her to stop doing what she's done and to continue to be your company. This shows you aren't able to find other ways of filling your schedule and being responsive to changes. Be positive and let her be. Playfully asking her to reschedule is a good way to flirt with her but not because you want her change her plans.

It can be hard to deal with repeated cancellations. Some ladies have a difficult time managing the initial stages of a relationship. It is heartbreaking to hear her excuses. For instance, she may claim she is going to bed early and will not be coming on the date.

She could have told you to get up earlier but it is not necessary. Remain positive, as the attraction of beauty requires patience, perseverance, self-control and a high level. You can make it your responsibility to cancel any plans she has been making.

In such cases, it is important to tell her that she can take as long as she wants and that you are happy for her. However, you want to be able to have a great time with her on your first date. You can keep the text conversation open by asking her to let your text know when she is available so you can grab some drinks with her. I wish her a happy evening and a fun day.

Sometimes men mistakenly believe that texting will make a girl notice how much they need you. Sometimes, this isn't the case. Women, especially professional players, can give you trouble and if they are soft-hearted, they will give up.

Although you may love the cute girls, don't let your texts show that you are desperate. It is different from calling. Texting isn't the same thing. If she is asking for advice, the texts you send her will be perfect material. Do not chase her with messages that are too personal or show you are thinking about her.

You will be seen as being immature if you are angry with her for cancelling a date several times. It can make girls turn off. In order to convince a girl to come to your house, you should avoid using text messages to guilt-trip her. You know she has cancelled several times, so respect your ego. Don't follow her too closely. That will make her realize that you also have standards. Doing so will put the ball in her court, and you'll wait for her texting to resume.

Breaking the silence The tactic described above, which is to keep quiet and allow her to come to you, will lead to the point that you will need to text her to rekindle that conversation.

They are wired differently and girls will not hold back for long. You are the one that is supposed to start a conversation. There will be times when the man has to return and check on the girl's progress. Do not be surprised that it will happen to him.

This should not be a reason to feel ashamed. You can also do it professionally. Some people restart the conversation by texting and ignoring their recipient. It is possible to ask the lady, "Hey, June's number?". This can really hurt her. It is because it makes her feel like you are treating her as a stranger, and she will be unable to remember who you are. She will feel that you are trying check for the owner of the unknown number in your telephone book.

One example of how it should be done is...

You should rekindle the conversation in a way that reminds her of the wonderful things you did together if they had ever met. She may have met another guy while you were gone, and you might now be up against more competition. You need to start the conversation on the right footing so that she will respond to your compliment.

Next, tell her why you are texting her. She will be interested in your story and ask you questions about how you came to remember her. Text her to let her know that you care about her. You can also text her to tell her that you were thinking of her. Honesty wins most women's hearts. When she sees you are being truthful, they will automatically consider you a friend.

Finally, if a girl is busy and seems to never have time for a date, be kind and let her know that you value her work as much as your own. Don't feel bad that she is busy.

Demonstrate to her how awesome it is to be productive and she'll be able to accomplish the tasks with ease. Each challenge that she presents you with should be used as an opportunity for you to pull her toward you. Tell her how easy it is for her to complete the assignment and ask her how she would enjoy celebrating her accomplishment. The final step is to ask her out for dinner, or a cup coffee. You will gauge her response during the texting process and determine if it's a winning situation.

Chapter 15: How To Unlock His Texting Codes

It is great to have someone to talk to and text with about your life, and other topics. Sometimes, we may misunderstand someone's messages and miss the true meaning of their words. Text messages can be one way to express interest between two people.

It is common to become obsessed with the messages sent by a guy after you have gone out with him. These text messages will be shared with your friends for their feedback and clarification. You want to make sure you have someone to explain it to to avoid any misinterpretations. You may find yourself thinking about every little thing he does. To get an additional opinion, you can send your friends the details of what you are going to reply. All that is fine. But, don't waste time or energy on your phone. Real men won't mind if you send them text messages.

Your communication habits should change when you begin to text someone. Men and women both change their texting habits once they start feeling connected. You can imagine how excited it is to see your crush's name on your phone. It is the time that we invest in making our crushes the best version possible. We send messages to people that we are attracted to in a different way than those we send to people who have no interest. These are some methods to help men understand how they text each other.

1. He is more attentive

A good indicator of the interest a guy has in you is how long it takes for him to respond. Do they take 30 minutes, an hour, a day, or just a minute? (Lol) Can he concentrate? However, guys are less good at texting than women, but a guy who cares about you will make an effort to respond to your texts. If a guy gets a text message from a girl he likes, he will know how and what to reply. He won't wait long to answer it. He will respond quickly, unlike a friend text. He is familiar with the message he wishes to send and will respond quickly. If he is not available immediately and is busy, apologize to him and offer an explanation.

2. He loves constant communication.

o A guy who is interested in a girl will reply to all of her messages. This will keep the conversation going, no matter how annoying. He will talk to you about anything if they find you attractive. He will make you laugh with his texting.

o He will keep you laughing to keep the conversation going.

3. He tries to have a conversation every day.

If he likes to talk, a man will often try to start conversations every day. He doesn't care if you are busy or asleep as long as he sends you a message. He will continue to check his phone for you to reply.

O He may be busy all the day but when he finds the time, he will be checking up on you.

There is no set rule as to who should first text, but girls can text men too. A guy who likes to chat with you will always text you first. Guys don't waste any time texting girls they do not like. Girls, check to see if your man is texting at all. He might believe you are not affected.

4. He drops hints

o He likes your text messages and will send them to you at a certain frequency.

If he is interested in you, he might even flirt with a little. If he doesn't want to talk to you, then he will limit the amount of communication he can have with you.

5. He starts to think about everything.

o He is curious about you and will spend a lot of time analysing and overanalyzing your messages.

o He doesn't want to offend or misunderstand you. A man who likes you will want to ensure that he provides a correct and satisfying answer.

o He will literally read out a reply loudly to make sure it sounds right before he sends it.

6. He carefully examines the last text sent.

o A man who isn't interested will stop you talking.

A guy who is interested in you will expect his texting to be back to back. If he's constantly addressing the previous text and sending a follow up to get an answer, then it's likely to make him feel disinterested.

7. He uses more of an filter.

o He will always send what he thinks you'd like.

o He will be more careful about what he says to your to avoid annoying you or to put you off.

o When it's early, he will try to please you. Later, when he is more familiar with you, he may not.

o He won't be annoying, nagging, or needy.

o He wants his best self to be available for you in his texts.

8. He keeps the conversation alive

o A guy who likes to talk with you will be able to keep the conversation going and come up with new topics. He might also want to go out for a drink with you.

o He will take any excuse to meet you for a one-on one conversation.

o He wants you to talk to him all the time. Even when the conversation has come to an abrupt halt, he will still find new topics to continue the conversation.

9. He is nervous when you respond to him

o The courting time is a key part of the relationship. Since he is not sure of your feelings about him, a man will be shy to reply to a text. His writings convey suggestive messages, but conceal them in his book. His version is more forward-looking, but will be respectful. He is nervous even when he is with his friends. He might even choose to walk away from you to read and respond to your text. He will simply text you and then close his phone until he feels strong enough to read your reply.

10. Ask personal questions

Unless he's interested in your interests, he won't be concerned with specific details. If he likes your personality, he will ask questions about you and get to know more.

o He wants to get to know you better to find out what you have going on.

o He will be open to sharing his sensory experiences and personal information, as it feels good to chat with you. When he is sharing, he will show that a lot of his feelings are open with you. He will talk to you when he is sharing, which could be an indication that he loves you.

o He will inquire about your family and ask about your friends. If we are sharing information about family with another person, we know it's serious.

11. Long texts

o The guys are lazy in texting and will avoid long texts. They prefer to use shorter forms of texting. They might even refuse to text back if they're not interested. Girl, if you get a longer text than normal, it means that the guy is interested in you. Because he is interested, he will send long text messages full of information to keep the conversation going. A guy who doesn't want to text you would not send you a lengthy message.

12. Send sweet messages via text every day, 24/7

o If you wake up to a sweet note from him, such as "Good morning Beautiful" or "Sleep Well Pretty", then it is a sign that he likes and values you. He wants to keep your thoughts on him throughout the day, and even before you go to bed.

13. 13. Random flirty emojis

o A guy who loves you will make sure that you know it by sending flirty emojis. He may randomly text you with kisses, heart emojis, winks, and smiles. This is not something guys will send to their friends. Take it as an honor to get them.

o He will sometimes try to tease with you with goofy GIFs or emojis.

o He wants it to be clear that he is interested in you, and he would like for you to feel the same.

14. 14. He talks about himself

o Don't be surprised if he speaks too much about himself or his interests. He wants you get to know him and love him. He already likes to be with you. All he wants from you is for you understand that and love him more.

o He may randomly send you such messages to get your attention or because he loves sharing with you.

15. 15. Random compliments

o You randomly get a text from him every day telling you how talented, beautiful, or funny it is. It's okay, girl. He doesn't do this without a reason. He clearly cares about you. He wants you feeling good about yourself. It is easy to assume that these messages are intended to make you feel better, but it is possible to quickly discern if his intentions are genuine. Do not assume that he is trying to impress you with insincere compliments. You might be wrong to judge him.

16. 16. Texting random stuff

It's not just about texting 'hello' and 'how are you?'. Exchanging your opinion on random stuff is the best way for you to see if there's anything in common.

o A guy who is interested in you may send you random information to begin a conversation. He might want to tell you something because he misses and needs to talk to me, or it could be something that interests his, and he hopes it will interest you.

Random topics are more attractive than normal conversations. These random texts may even make you more attractive to him.

17. He loves to make plans

o A guy who is interested in you will often ask about your weekly plans. He likes to spend time with your because he loves spending time with them.

o He will take u to a coffee, dinner or other special occasion.

If you do not have time to go, he may ask for your permission.

o He will randomly visit to bring you movies or snacks.

18. Double-checking texts is not an option

o Men should not text twice if they forget something. He does not want to make you look desperate or scare him away.

You don't need to worry if a guy sends you double the amount of text messages.

If you get a constant buzzing sound from your phone's messages, it's probably because he is really interested in you.

19. Inside jokes

o A sense a humor is the best way of connecting, especially if the two of you have your inside jokes. You can make jokes that aren't funny, but only you and your partner will hear them. If you have inside jokes that you enjoy with a guy, it's probably because he likes your jokes.

20. He will give you adorable nicknames

A nickname is a way for a guy to call you. He will use it frequently to show his interest. It allows him to be closer to you, and it can also help them express their intimacy. It is also charming.

o Nicknames may be given to friends by a guy, but they don't have the same meaning as yours.

21. Texts like "If you were there ...'

If the next part is sexual, this text could be uncanny. Instead, a man who is in you will propose things that you could do together. For example, playing games with your friends, going out for drinks, and watching movies. It is clear that he wants to spend quality time with and get to know you better. Because he likes your company, he is doing all of this.

22. He appreciates you sharing your thoughts and offering advice.

o Men like to seek advice from people they trust when they are unsure of something. He turns to his closest friend for support when he doesn't agree with his family and friends. He needs sound advice and understanding at the moment. Likeable men will seek your guidance on details such as selecting the right attire for a certain occasion. He appreciates your support and will trust that you will offer honest advice.

23. Asking for a picture of you

He loves to take selfies of you even when you are not there. He loves to smile, look at your photos and admire your beauty. It's those photos that bring joy to his heart. Many compliments will come from him, praising you for being beautiful and describing your perfect self. He will be more impressed if you keep your natural appearance, which I'm sure he enjoys. He will hold your photo on his smartphone to feel your presence. If he misses your presence, he will see that photo on his phone. So send him that selfie girl.

24. Excellent spelling and punctuation

o Girls are more comfortable with long sentences than short messages. It sounds better when you write it in its entirety.

She wants to make sure you understand what she is referring to.

o If a guy is in love with a girl, he will put his best effort to type correct sentences. He knows that you're worth it and wants you to be impressed. Because he cares about you, he'll do anything to make an impression.

25. Guys texting, "I like your"

o If he sends you messages like "you're hilarious, and I really like" or "you make you so happy, that's what I like about you", you might get indirect hints that it is him who likes you. The guy is trying to send you some secret messages. You should not stop texting him even after the message, until you are certain of his feelings. But I think he really loves you.

26. Random texts

A random text from a guy you love is the best thing. A random text comes from him, even if you're bored at work. It feels so good. But, you know what? He has a reason. And it is you. He did this because he likes you and enjoys messaging with you.

o This is not a normal behavior for guys. They rarely text their friends. It only means that he likes you.

27. Drunk guys send honest messages

* Men will say things that they would not when they are sober to women they like when they are drunk. You shouldn't panic or get mad if you receive a text message from the drunk man stating that he wants your attention. You don't have to worry about him forgetting the text. Maybe he will remember your good morning message and read some of his messages. He might ignore it. But, what

is most important is that you now know the truth.

Many people believe that women are more complicated than men, but it's not true. It's difficult to text someone without knowing their facial expressions or body language. It is more difficult to read the messages if the man is not clear and concise. If you have to ask questions like does, it's likely that he actually thinks or means what you have been texting. If you've been texting and going out with a boy, these things will help to make sense of him and answer your many questions.

Chapter 16: Text Messaging Rules

You should, just like with all acts, have a set list of rules you must follow when you text a guy. This will allow for smooth conversations and even a possible romance that can last a lifetime.

Several of the rules in this book have been covered before. Refer to the Table. If certain things have been mentioned before in this book, which is likely to be repeated, it means that they are important and should be remembered. It is important to remember this book with all your heart and soul. These will serve as your rules for engagement in the future.

Do

1. Be sweet and send him sweet words - let them know that you remembered this

day. It does not have to be reciprocated. You don't have to return the favor. Simple "hi sweetie", I hope you're having a great time. (See Building Attraction).

2. It is important to respond quickly - although it may appear confusing, early on we discussed not to be too eager. You should give him a minimum of one minute before you respond. Any more than that will be taken to signify that you aren't interested.

3. Before you actually meet him, text him. Have fun and keep it light. This will help calm his nerves and put him at ease.

4. KISS: Keep it short and simple. You are restricted to a maximum of 20 characters for text messages. It is important not to exceed this limit. Do not send too many messages. Allow for longer messages to be used in face-toface conversations.

5. Take care with your spelling and grammar. Your best self is not limited to face-to face interactions. Be aware of any typographical errors or grammar mistakes in your message. He wouldn't think less of your message and be more concerned about your mistakes if he did. (see Text Blunders).

Don't

1. Drink and Text - The danger of drinking while driving is nearly the same as that of drinking and sending a message. You may regret what you say the next morning. If you don't have the opportunity to undo what was done, avoid wine on a girls night out.

2. Texting should not be a game. It's not a way to play mind games with your guy. Be sincere when you say something. Do not try hard to get. You could send him

the wrong message and he might lose interest in you.

3. The argument can wait until you meet him face-to–face. Sometimes a message is perceived as offensive, even though it's not. Arguments over SMS are futile. Never quit using SMS. You may regret making the wrong decision when the fire dies down.

4. Texting for the sake or sending SMS should not be considered a job. It's okay to talk with him about your day, but what should you tell them about what you're having for lunch? To get an idea of the topics you might discuss, think about what you should text.

5. Learn to text and forget. - Conversation threads, sent items and messages were created for one purpose. This is to ensure you do not forget what you say, even if your response takes

longer than usual. You can text and forget. Don't be too obsessed with his response. Don't look at your phone blankly as if he is asking you to return the favor.

6. Do not regret something. Never. While some men might find it attractive, they may not take your seriousness seriously.

7. Don't finish any sentence with a "ha-ha", "he he," or "lol" - you don't want to make him laugh. You don't want him to believe you are laughing at and not with them.

Chapter 17: Mistakes – What Would My Younger Self Have Learned?

These were my mistakes before I had any idea of how to message a girl. Because it provides a quick and simple set of guidelines that you can use to text her, I included this chapter.

It is easier to read and understand by creating a list format.

My Biggest Mistakes in Starting Out

Missing the mark: Replying to ALL things - I made this mistake at least 95%. I was replying every single thing. If you've ever text a girl and got no reply to a question you had, it's likely that you felt "something". I am not talking about the girl texting you a plan and you ignoring them.

I focus on the little things. If she asks you a dumb question, such as about your car's specs, or if her joke isn't funny enough. Instead of replying with a sarcastic reply or humouring the question, what you should do is express your power to not respond every now and then. Do it because it is 'doing it'. Be a good judge of your abilities and do it when it makes sense.

You might be thinking this is incredibly rude. It's not so bad. But it's only when used properly.

Do you remember being on the receiving side of such an exchange? Maybe you were able to tell a dull joke or ask her a silly question but she did nothing. If that is the case, you will probably spend a lot of time wondering why her text didn't go back to you. And you may also wonder if she was doing something wrong.

We often spend way too much time thinking about it. If we are lucky enough to like the girl enough, sometimes we go into a denial stage where we assume she is very busy or that her phone has been messed-up.

Let's examine the facts. There could have been many positive outcomes for her. Many times, a girl will open a text message and not reply. However, they may have an idea of what they want to do right away. Five hours later, they forgot all about it.

Remember that you aren't the only guy there. She won't respond unless you are working to develop deeper feelings.

As I mentioned in the book, girls are different to men. You will be judged by her emotions, which can change over time. Guys are more comfortable with hot women who are not bummed than they are. This mentality is somewhat associated with women. It's do or die. She either likes you or not. This mentality is what leads to the death of so many good men.

It's her emotions which determine whether she likes you. However, you can change them if you ignite them. They can also change because they are a fluctuating variable. You can think of it as a volume control.

This brings us back to our initial point. You don't have to respond to all messages. It is okay to not always respond, but it is a good thing to do if you are a fan. If she asks you a stupid question or tells you a joke that isn't funny, don't answer. This causes her to second guess herself. Overthinking things can lead to her subconsciously thinking that you are of higher status than herself. If you recall what we spoke about earlier, higher status = attractive.

2. Mistake #2: Persistence Yes. Neediness NO

This is what I mean. This is the scenario:

Let's imagine you ask her to come to your house tonight. She will reply with "ehh"

You might then be able to suggest a quick getaway together. You will pick her and get a cup of tea or run to the local grocery store. This takes some perseverance.

She said no because she hasn't seen you yet.

You tease the girl a bit, saying that she is not adventurous or 'lame' or boring'. Another hint: her friend should meet you. Another good example of persistency is shown here.

Although she loves to be seen, she just doesn't want anything to do tonight.

You tell her it's okay and she shouldn't be worried.

Now imagine it happening again. Every time she asked you for something, she replied with something. It could mean that she doesn't like you. But you won't like to think that way. Attraction is just a knob that can be turned by the right emotions you bring to her. Do not be dependent on her.

This is a common response from men. They might ask "does your girlfriend even want to meet me?" or push their way too far and make it clear that they need other men. One of the most unattractive characteristics for women is when they are sexy. Make mistake #2: It is okay to be persistent in a light-hearted way that is fun and not too serious, but it shouldn't become needy.

Third Mistake: Be completely Different from Text

This can make it difficult for her to trust you. It's not uncommon. Here's an example.

Let's imagine you are out with your girlfriend. This may not be a first date. It could be work or school. The average nice guy won't ask her out in real life because that could make her uncomfortable. So, the nice guy just asks her to text. Also, the nice guy only speaks dirty via text.

A lack of consistency can make you seem a little sloppy and show her that you're not confident. Confidence is a key factor in attracting women to a man.

With mistake #3, the key is to ask yourself "Is it consistent with how I act in real life?"

Chapter 18: Sexing: Do's And Don'ts

Sexting should be avoided unless you have had actual sex or are initiated by a woman. I would advise against sexting. There are exceptions, of course. If she is sending nude photos of her self to your phone, then you can go ahead. It's best to wait until you have established a sexual relationship before initiating it.

It is not because you want to be nice but because it will lead to the opposite result to what you desire. Women will only sex with men with whom they feel secure and comfortable. Be too strong and you will make her feel uncomfortable. Even if she does respond to your request, it is likely that you have done more harm than you have done to increase your chances of her getting laid.

A sexual undertone is different from adding one. While good flirting can create a sense of sexual tension, it doesn't mean you have to treat her as if she were a meat. You can make her desirable without having to make observations about her body.

Set some Standards

Harvard and Princeton are considered prestigious schools because of their exclusivity. Because not everyone can apply, this makes them more desirable and attracts more people. They have high standards that are unique among other schools. These high standards do not drive people away. Instead, they draw them closer.

When you seduce a woman, the same principle applies. In order to make her want to date you, you must also show that you have certain standards. While you don't have to make it so explicit, you must convey the fact that you will not be just dating any girl who offers their number. Your standards will help you make her feel better. It's like when someone is admitted to an Ivy League university. Because it was difficult, we feel more pride than if it were easy.

A way to demonstrate your standards is by asking her the so-called qualifying questions. These questions don't have the need to be serious as you aren't trying to vet her. Although the qualifiers are funny, they help set standards that she has to meet. You could say, "I wouldn't date a woman that my dog doesn't like." It's a ridiculous test, but it's worth the effort. If she's interested, she'll be nervous about whether she'll get along with your dog. By stating your standards, you are demonstrating that you don't want to lower them.

Last Minute Dates to Accept

You shouldn't accept any invitations she sends you to go out on a date last-minute. Doing so will diminish your value. This is generally true and should be observed. If she asks for you to go out right away, tell her that she is already busy. Schedule a time when she is available.

But there are exceptions. It's okay to accept a friend's invitation if you're out with friends at clubs on Saturday night. You will be in a stronger position if you invite someone to join you at whatever event you are involved in. Do not be seen as running away each time she calls.

However, Saturday night is a great opportunity to get together and if she appears interested, then do it. Remember to be honest and not seem like you are doing anything else with your time.

Chapter 19: What Is Entitlement?

It is possible that she will ignore you at times during the texting process. It's a good idea for her to respond at least once. Who knows?

A 'no' is a sign of non-compliance. It means the conversation or interaction has stopped progressing. This means you have to go backwards in order fix it. This could be a sign that you didn't add enough value or offer enough comfort.

You're not sure how to go about following up with the girl, because the interaction didn't go according to plan.

What is entitlement?

Remember that a girl doesn't owe either you or her anything when you follow-up with her.

Actually, you both can decide to leave the text as is. Both you and she are potentially offering each other a great experience. But neither of you is obliged to do anything.

One common error when responding to silences is to either display too much entitlement or too little entitlement. It will depend on the stage of your process as to how much entitlement is available. Let's examine a few scenarios.

Scenario 1: She ignores your first text message

Let's imagine that you send the best opening line possible and the girl doesn't respond. Maybe she didn't see it or was too busy responding at the time. The most common mistake men make is to feel too entitled and then get frustrated when the girl does not reply.

A bad thing to say is "what's there in matching with me?" or "what's your point in giving my number if no one replies?" This is a show of entitlement and neediness.

Humour is a more effective way to handle this situation. It could be something as simple as "silence, is sexy", or "I like when girls play hard for me" or something more cheeky that shows you aren't afraid to say what you think.

Scenario 2. You are texting back-and-forth, but she suddenly stops messaging.

If you have a good relationship with her in the past, you can simply ignore the fact that your message was not received and assume that she actually forgot it. This will show her that you have enough entitlement.

In this instance, it is best to assume that she forgot and just carry on as usual. This will give her an excuse to say she didn't get your message. Sometimes girls may feel rude if they do not reply after a few days.

Your follow up message shouldn't highlight that she ignored your messages or ask if everything is okay. It should not be a formal follow up message. Pictures are a great way of ending the non-response, e.g. It could be something you did, cooked, or something else you witnessed that day. If she likes enough of you, she'll likely be polite enough to say "wow that is awesome" and then apologise for not replying.

Scenario #3: She is always responsive to your inquiries, but she is never interested meeting up.

The situation where the girl refuses to meet you up is quite common. It could be either she wants to be a text buddy or she is uncomfortable with the idea of meeting up.

You should work hard to distance from her if she is using your emotional comfort or just wants your attention. If she is persistent in her pursuit of you, you should follow the seeding the close process. If she insists on saying 'no', it is time to move on. She has no intention of meeting with you.

If she doesn't respond or keeps talking, it could mean you haven't developed enough intimacy. To fix this problem quickly, call her. This is the ultimate test. Because it's safer and easier for girls to text than do this, guys should not do it anymore.

If she answers the phone, or calls you back, then you can try to set up the next appointment. Simply calling her will make it more attractive. Why is this possible? Because texting back is tedious and repetitive. By calling her, you're being more attractive.

Scenario 4. She agrees that she will meet up, but then cancels at last minute

Another possibility is for her to agree to the first date, but then she backs out last-minute with an excuse such as she's too tired, too busy, or the weather isn't cooperating. Are these legitimate reasons or is she simply trying to make excuses for not meeting up?

If she cancels, but then she offers another date to you, it is possible she is still interested. You should be wary if she keeps cancelling, putting you off or cancelling. Don't be discouraged if she keeps giving vague answers like "I will let you know", or "next weeks" then it is likely that she is not interested in you. Because they feel awkward rejecting a man, girls do this.

If she has a valid reason to not agree to your date, you can work with her to find out what it is. If she states that she suffers from cold and doesn't want to go out in the rain, it is possible to change the date to a dinner at a warm place and promise to give her your jacket.

If she tells you she's too busy, then you might suggest that she has a low-intensive date like a coffee or a walk around her neighborhood during her lunch break. If she says she cannot refuse, then she is not interested. If she is in love with you enough, she will find time to spend time with you.

Scenario 5

If you and your partner have made tentative plans to meet, but you are having difficulty setting up the exact date or time, this is a situation where you can both be friends. In this instance, you don't need to start the process over. This will make it look like you are low value as you don't think the plan will work.

It is best to act the same way you would if you were planning something with a friend. If you reach the stage of making solid plans, then you have enough rapport and you've had an enjoyable interaction.

It's possible to send something like a "..." question mark or "you leave me hanging here" (laughing) to let her know that you're expecting a reply. This is a way to communicate to the girl that she is not responding to your messages and that you expect her to reply. Because you've already reached a significant point in the process, this is only appropriate.

Scenario 6

Let's assume, for example that you have already set a date and time. If she doesn't respond to your request, it's too close.

In such a case, it is best to not ask her "are there still meetings up?". This shows low value behavior as it implies that you don't think you are going meet up. It may also allow her to change her mind.

Instead, you can just send a brief statement to let her know that you're on your route or your ETA a few days before the date. This will let her know that the date has been set and it will also assure her that you will be there. It's not trying to appear pushy or needy.

Chapter 20: You Will Make Her Love You By Your Wonderful Texts.

Complacency is the most common mistake made when texting. Complacency is the biggest mistake people make in texting. She is not a piece of furniture. You must think about her in a fun, positive, caring way that is kind, loving, and important.

Make your texts exciting and interesting. You don't have to be juicy hot because that depends on where your texting game is at the moment, but you should be interesting hot. It is nice to send an occasional good night or morning message. It's great to send random texts to your partner about what you both hope to do together one day, what you would like for them to do together one day, or even to mention travel.

* "Hey Sarah. Instead of working, I am looking at a Europe travel brochure. We might one day be able to travel around Italy by backpacking!

* "I am doing science, but instead I feel that we should spend the weekend together going to New York's museums. Sarah, what do you think?

* "Sarah. Did you know about this new Italian restaurant that opened in my community? The pasta is hand made, perhaps that's where you should go for your first date.

You will notice that the guy has named the girl in all three of the above texts. He hasn't called her.

* Sweetheart

* Baby

* Honey

*

* Sugar.

It is important for girls to be called intelligent, sophisticated and stylish. They are also happy to be called by the real names of their partners and prefer to be called nicknames only once they have established a connection. It's not a good idea to text your girl and make up a nickname for her, Cookie, etc. Be sure to get to know one another before you start looking for pet names.

She will also likely to block you if your name is Cookie.

You can personalize your messages by using someone's first name. It makes them seem more intimate and personal. That intimate point is what you want, don't ya? Use her name.

Complacency can also cause people to become lazy in their grammar and spelling. Don't do it. Use proper punctuation and spelling. Although you can do it, especially if the recipient is young, use SMH, ROFL and STFU. It is lazy, painstaking and not very intellectual. Unless she texts you this way, then you shouldn't mind. If she does, then feel free!

Mirror Texting lets you take your cues directly from her. You can also send her tons and tons of emoji if she loves to send you emoji.

If you prefer emojis over words, feel free to use as many of the emoji you like. If she doesn't use emoji often, you can follow her example. If she replies to your messages within seconds, you should follow her lead. Don't wait for her to reply to your messages every time.

Instead, try to get her to respond faster by being a smarter texter. She might not be interested but you can still get her to take an interest in you.

Don't be an everlasting joker. She will be more entertained than laughing at your jokes. It's not your intention to be rude or crass. Rather, you want to make the woman smile and laugh in an almost flirtatious manner. You don't want the response to be an awkward eye roll. You want it to be a frowning of the eyes.

Always remember to be sweet to her. Be honest and true. Sweet texts can brighten her day and make her feel good. They will help her see that you have an emotional side and a sweet side. You could also try these sweet texts:

* "Been thinking about you all the day."

* "I understand you are busy. I just wanted to send you a quick hello and a small hug."

* "You're very special to my heart and I love talking about you. Chat later ..."

* "You make it feel good. I want to do the same thing for you."

* "Missing you and your dog!"

All the text above is honest. These are not messages where you want to make a big deal or score points. You are being true to yourself.

When asked by girls which text messages they are most excited to receive, their answers will be:

* Sweet, loving and kind texts

* You can have fun with short texts and emojis

* Texts to make us feel good.

* Texts that show how the guy drives.

* Texts that have not been edited.

* Meaningful texts

They'll also tell you they don't like to be overwhelmed by texts. Begin to text a girl when you are just getting started. It's easy to feel like you're the only girl in the universe and have an intense crush on her. However, if you start sending her too many messages at once, she may find it too overwhelming and block your attempts. You can slow down, remind her of kindness and respect, and also show your good side.

There's also the concept of'showing' rather than telling. Although you can communicate to a girl by text that your are funny, active, or entertaining, it can also be seen as bragging. Braggers don't like being irritated, and nobody likes braggers. You can text her, but you should also try to show her. Here are some examples of showing and not telling.

"Hiya Suzie. I love to cook, so I have invited a few people to my house for Friday night. I would love for you to join us all but me.

The last line with the 'especially me,' shows that you are more in love with her than a close friend.

You might also find that a simple hello or hiya is more pleasant than a more formal hello.

To show her that you are passionate about something, another way is to:

* "Hey. I'm looking for a good thriller and just finished my novel. I know you enjoy reading so, any suggestions?

* "It's the Oscars Sunday night, and I think you share a love for movies. Would you like us to watch together? We could even dress up to drink champagne.

This text is very special because it shows her that you like movies and that you want to spend some time with her.

You should also remember not to send anything that could be considered racist, sexist, prejudicial or judgmental when sending text messages. Different opinions might exist about what is appropriate. As you get to understand each other, you can see the potential offenses. Don't be offensive

It is important to keep your photographs safe. But, that doesn't mean you shouldn't have fun or flirt. It is essential that you let her know how much you love her. Be you and be fun. Be a wonderful listener. If she asks to send you a picture she took in her new gown, say yes! Don't send inappropriate photos. That is crass, and it will come back to bite. After a while or after a few dates you may want to share some saucy pics with one another. This is something you should always be aware of and encourage your partner to do. She will appreciate you taking care of her.

Do not forget to surprise the girl who you like from time-to-time. You don't need to send flowers as an emoji. Send her flowers in a full bouquet.

If you don't want to spend a lot, you can still buy flowers and drop them at her school. You could send her a photo of a wineglass, a lobster, and a smile to go out with her on a date. Sending her an emoji that looks like an aubergine will not be a good idea. If you wish to take her to the beaches, send a message that reads 'beach?' and includes an emoji representing the ocean with an umbrella.

Try something different with your texting. Keep her surprised and happy and she will keep coming back.

Chapter 21: Important Things To Consider When Texting

Here are some additional points to consider when messaging women.

You can edit your text messages and hide your facial expressions. However, it is better to be truthful and honest than to go over your entire life. It allows you to modify what you're saying before it is said and does not allow you to pretend you're someone else. To create genuine and nice phrases, you can text.

Be you and keep it real. The best way to find the right partner for you is to not pretend to be somebody else. It's easy to pretend you are likable or loved in text messages. But it's better to present yourself in person.

You must be sincere but still polite. It is communicating what you are trying to communicate in a way that does not offend the other person.

It's not necessary that you look desperate to receive a reply every day. You need to demonstrate that you still have a daily life beyond texting. You must continue with your normal activities and allow texting to be used in moderation. A woman won't accept a man who texts only during the day.

It's better to discuss future plans on dates than when they are being discussed. Your expression is what women want to see when you discuss these topics. It is a great way to show her your sincerity.

Text messaging is great for communicating with people and keeping in touch. However, it is important to continue using other forms of communication. A text conversation cannot replace a real date. Being together in person strengthens a relationship.

Chapter 22: The Psychology Behind Texting

"The pen is stronger than the sword," Edward Bulwer Lytton used that phrase to describe his play "Richelieu, or, the Conspiracy". He didn't realize how powerful it would be almost 180 years later.

Because of the speed and ease with which we communicate, many people forget just how powerful their words can be. It is easy to forget that words can have a profound effect on someone's life, whether or not we intend to. Most emails and texts are sent without the same level of thought and planning that we used to have back when ink was first printed.

There are also certain things that are more likely to be communicated to someone by text than what we would normally say to them in person. Because of the extra space texting gives us, and the recipient, this is possible. It removes the anxiety and allows us be more direct, confident, and less anxious about asking for or saying something. Texting, in effect is an electronic version of the old-fashioned mask that we wear.

Numerous psychiatrists have found texting to help them understand their patients' issues. In this instance, the patient sends a short text message to the psychiatrist at the time they are experiencing a problem. It eliminates any risk of the patient losing important information as they don't need to rely on their memory when sharing their problems with the psychiatrist. The patient is able to be more honest because there is no anxiety. Patients are more likely to text to confess to mistakes they made and things they regret. This is especially true of teenagers who experimented with illegal drugs.

A significant role has also been played by texting in romantic relationships. Many couples use it as a way to communicate. Teenagers are more inclined to texting their love interests about 30 times per hour. This is according to a teenager study. These men and women (and those of the next generation) have grown to texting to be socially acceptable ways to communicate with romantic partners.

Is texting healthy in a relationship?

Although texting isn't a replacement for personal communication, it can certainly have its advantages. First, because it is human nature that we follow the path of least resistance (texting), texting can be much easier than having personal conversations. Second, you don't have worry about whether or not you are clever enough. There is more time for cleverly-formulated quips in texting than there would be in direct conversation.

Also, body language can't be sent over text messages. Therefore, there's no danger of another person seeing your nervousness as sweaty hands or nervous twitches.

Interjections like "ummm", or "like" are annoying in conversation. They make us appear less confident and persuasive. This is not the case with texting.

To help reduce the chance of rejection, texting can be very helpful. It allows you to find out if someone that you've met may be interested. Most people who meet in person will try to find out more about one another through social networking. Once they have established a connection, the first communication will be via the social media platform.

After that, it is possible for one of them to ask the other's number. This will result in texting and eventually a actual date.

Once you have established a relationship with someone, it's important to decide how much of your texting preferences you would like to use. The more text messages they are received, the more people feel obligated to respond. This could be healthy, provided that there isn't a feeling of dependency. Problems can arise if a person is not able to fulfill other obligations or personal responsibilities, and a lot of texts are sent.

While texting can be a good way to hide your body language at first, it can also cause misinterpretations and misunderstandings within a relationship.

Human communication relies on facial expressions and vocal nuances. We can't communicate a lot if we don't use facial expressions, nuances and tone of voice. These, along with the psychological distance texting creates can quickly lead anxiety and ambivalence.

Texting can also help to create stability and contentment in a relationship. Studies show that heterosexual partners who text more often have happier relationships. It is a sign that a romantic partner is happier if they text less often than men. Strangely, however, men who text to express affection tend to have partners who feel a stronger sense of attachment.

If you want your relationship to be successful, it is crucial to have clear rules about texting. One thing is certain: you should never allow texting to be your main means of communication.

Chapter 23: Maintaining The Conversation

Now, you have made it through the initial contact. It is great. A new texting conversation's opening lines can be awkward and difficult. Everyone sends texts in a different way. You want to let your sarcasm show through but also show him that you are kind and flirty. It's now time to keep in touch with him. That doesn't mean that you have to stay in touch with your friend every day. You just need to be able and willing to engage with him when it suits you. It is important to remember that conversations do not go in circles. Instead it reveals different truths which allows you to build and sustain communication. This requires you to be honest and sincere. Be honest and sincere. You can then move the conversation to a point where you can ask him if they would like to go out to eat so that your mind is not on work. Being sincere is a sign of respect and authenticity. You can cut the crap by knowing they can handle what you really feel. Being honest is not something that can be done by anyone. You can't be honest without adding tension and grit to the conversation. You want to find out how he feels about different situations, what are his passions, what are his likes/dislikes, and how you could work together. It is important to ask clear, concise, but engaging questions in order to achieve this. You will need to practice this technique a lot, but eventually you will be able to do it. You can open the Word Document again, cut out half of the words, and see if it sounds too long. Is he going to see it? What would he think? Or that he cares about your life?

You must make an effort to embrace him once he opens up. As you move toward a more intimate relationship (which will be discussed in the next chapter), make sure you acknowledge him for sharing what he truly feels. It's okay to not make him feel awkward, but let him know that it was a great conversation. Because he had such a great conversation with you, he will realize how much he needs to talk to you and share his heart.

Let the conversation flow naturally. You don't have to go after him every day. Just text him when it feels necessary. He is probably annoyed by the constant stream of "Hey, What's Up" from girls. The other golden rule to texting is that men rarely text a lot. Let the conversation end if you don't feel like it is moving along. Don't forget, this is not a first meeting. You are simply sending him a letter. Keep it short. You want to be able to talk face-to–face with him. You can have more fun releasing tension by having conversations with him instead of focusing on the issues. Never lose sight of the goal.

It takes time and effort to maintain a conversation via text. You have to be patient and in the forefront of your conversation. Keep in mind that you don't have to text him every hour. He will still be able to understand if you can go a week and not say anything. He hasn't forgotten about you. But, most importantly, show genuineness. Asking him about his day will allow you to express your emotions and show sincerity. You want to get closer to him. Do not be afraid, nobody likes emotional sluts, but do not be afraid, let him know what you think about that dinner. He will respect you for trusting him. And when

you sit down face-to face, it will create a
sense of connection and mutual respect.

Conclusion

Texting can be a powerful method of communicating and, with today's modern gadgets, it is easy to communicate fluently, constantly, every second. If you want to court women. You just need to get her number. Soon you'll be exchanging wonderful words and leading to a blooming relationship.

Text messaging is an excellent way to communicate. It allows you to be as precise as possible before you transmit your message.

This guideline will help make the most of the messaging. It will allow you to win the heart the woman you're attracted to without having to step foot outside your house. Try your luck today!